UNLOCKING ONLINE WEALTH:

STRATEGIES FOR MAKING MILLIONS ONLINE

© **Pd John**

Copyright

All rights reserved, it is not permitted to copy, reprint or duplicate this book without the permission of the author.

Major Prophet PD John
P.O. BOX 4016
Mwanza - Tanzania
Phone number:
+255 762 415 790/ +255 759 204 744
Yohanayona3@gmail.com
www.hl centre.info

ISBN : 9798329083996
First edition ©2024.
Imprint: Independently published

Chief Editor:
Josia pd John
josiajohn735@gmail.com
Dar es salaam - Tanzania
Tel: +255 758588127/ +255 693522834

Unlocking Online Wealth: Strategies for Making Millions Online

Dedication:

To my dear grandmother, who always believed in me and encouraged me to chase my dreams. Thank you for instilling in me the importance of hard work and perseverance. This book is dedicated to you, as a testament to the wealth of knowledge and wisdom you have passed on to me. May it inspire others to unlock their own online wealth and achieve financial success.

Disclaimer:

The information provided in this ebook is for educational purposes only. The author and publisher are not responsible for any actions taken based on the content of this ebook. It is advised to consult with professionals and conduct thorough research before starting any online business venture.

Preface:

Welcome to "Unlocking Online Wealth: Strategies for Making Millions Online." In a world where the digital landscape is ever-expanding and opportunities abound, this book aims to be your guide to navigating the exciting realm of online entrepreneurship. Whether you're a seasoned business owner looking to expand your horizons or a budding entrepreneur eager to tap into the immense potential of the online world, this book is designed to provide you with the knowledge and strategies you need to thrive.

The power of the online world is undeniable. It has revolutionized the way we connect, communicate, and conduct business. The journey to online wealth is not just about financial gain, but also about embracing innovation, creativity, and the potential to impact lives globally.

In the following pages, you will embark on a journey that covers everything from laying a strong foundation for your online venture, building a solid online presence, diversifying your income streams, scaling your business, and cultivating the right mindset for success. From identifying lucrative niches to harnessing the power of social media, from monetizing through various strategies to navigating legal and ethical considerations – this book is your comprehensive roadmap.

However, it's important to remember that while this book provides valuable insights, it's not a guaranteed shortcut to overnight success. Building an online empire requires dedication, perseverance, and continuous learning. It's a journey filled with challenges and triumphs, setbacks and breakthroughs. The online world is dynamic, and staying ahead of the curve requires adaptability and an eagerness to embrace change.

As you delve into the chapters ahead, keep in mind that every step you take, every strategy you implement, is a part of your unique journey. Embrace the knowledge shared here, but also explore and experiment with your own ideas. Seek inspiration, collaborate with others, and never underestimate the power of your own creativity.

Lastly, remember that while this book provides guidance, your success ultimately lies in your hands. The strategies presented here are tools in your arsenal, and how you wield them will determine your outcomes. So, embark on this journey with an open mind, a willingness to learn, and an unwavering commitment to your dreams.

Your journey to unlocking online wealth begins now. Let's navigate this exciting landscape together and pave the way for your online success.

Best wishes on your entrepreneurial adventure,

[Prophet PD John]

My Testimony

As a pastor of a small church, I have always been passionate about sharing the word of God and helping others in their spiritual journey. However, pastoring a church comes with many financial restraints. With a modest salary and limited resources, I often found myself struggling to make ends meet and provide for my family.

It was during one particularly challenging time that I began to explore opportunities for additional income. I had heard about the potential of making money online and decided to venture into the world of online business as a side hustle. Little did I know that this decision would not only help alleviate my financial burden but also open up a whole new world of possibilities for me.

I started by researching different online business models and strategies for making money on the internet. I read books, attended webinars, and sought advice from experts in the field. I soon realized that there were countless opportunities to generate income online, from e-commerce and affiliate marketing to online coaching and consulting.

After much contemplation, I decided to start an e-commerce business selling handmade goods. I leveraged my passion for crafting and creativity to create unique products that resonated with customers. I set up an online store, optimized my website for search engines, and promoted my products through social media and email marketing.

To my surprise, my online business began to take off. Orders started pouring in, and I soon found myself juggling my responsibilities as a pastor with the demands of running a successful online business. While it was a lot of work and required long hours of dedication, the rewards were well worth it.

Not only did my online business provide me with a supplemental income, but it also allowed me to reach a wider audience and impact more lives. Through my online store, I was able to connect with customers from around the world, share my faith, and inspire others with my story.

As my online business continued to grow, I began to explore new opportunities for expansion. I diversified my product line, collaborated with other entrepreneurs, and invested in online advertising to reach a larger audience. I also started offering online courses and workshops to share my knowledge and expertise with others who wanted to start their own online businesses.

Through hard work, perseverance, and a willingness to learn, my side hustle soon transformed into a thriving online business that generated a significant income. I was able to pay off debts, save for the future, and even support my church and community through charitable donations.

Today, as I reflect on my journey as both a pastor and an online entrepreneur, I am filled with gratitude for the opportunities that have come my *way. My online business has not only provided me with financial stability but also a sense of fulfillment and purpose. I am grateful for the lessons I have learned, the challenges I have overcome, and the blessings that have been bestowed upon me.*

In conclusion, my experience of unlocking online wealth has been nothing short of transformative. It has empowered me to dream bigger, take risks, and pursue my passions with courage and determination. I hope that my story serves as inspiration for others who may be facing financial restraints and looking for a way to achieve financial success online. With the right mindset, determination, and a willingness to learn, anything is possible. So go ahead, unlock your own online wealth and make millions online.

Table of Contents:

Copyright I

Dedication: III

Disclaimer: IV

Preface: V

My Testimony VIII

Table of Contents: XII

Chapter 1: Introduction 1

    Unleashing the Potential of the Digital Frontier 1

    Navigating the Digital Landscape 2

    The Promise of Online Wealth 2

    A Roadmap to Success 3

    The Caveats and Considerations 3

    Embarking on a Transformative Journey 4

Chapter 2: Setting the Foundation: Navigating the Digital Frontier of Online Business 5

2.1 The Evolution of Online Entrepreneurship: A Modern Exodus 5

2.2 Identifying Lucrative Online Niches: Finding Your Digital Promised Land 8

2.3 The Importance of Keyword Research: Digital Stones of Success 13

Crafting Your Online Path 16

Chapter 3: Building Your Online Empire Forging Essential Strategies in the Digital Realm 17

3.1 Creating a Strong Online Presence: Your Digital Pillar of Cloud and Fire 17

3.2 Developing a Profitable Website or Blog: Crafting Your Online Ark 21

3.3 Leveraging Social Media for Maximum Impact: The New Digital Marketplace 24

3.4 Email Marketing: The Key to Long-Term Success 28

3.5 Effective Search Engine Optimization (SEO) Techniques: Navigating the Digital Wilderness31

Pillars of Your Online Empire 35

Chapter 4: Monetizing Your Online Ventures - Forging Diverse Pathways to Financial Abundance 36

4.1 Affiliate Marketing: Earning Commissions36

4.2 Selling Digital Products: Crafting and Selling Your Digital Artifacts 39

4.3 Dropshipping: Curating an E-commerce Store without Inventory 42

4.4 Online Advertising: Maximizing Revenue through Digital Billboards 45

4.5 Freelancing and Consulting: Sharing Your Expertise 49

Pillars of Prosperity 53

Chapter 5: Scaling Your Online Business - Ascending to New Heights in the Digital Horizon 55

5.1 Outsourcing and Automation: Streamlining Operations 55

5.2 Expanding Your Reach: Targeting International Markets..................................58

5.3 Building a Brand: Establishing Trust and Credibility 64

5.4 Collaborations and Joint Ventures: Leveraging Partnerships..................................66

5.5 Continuous Learning: Staying Ahead in the Online World 69

Climbing to New Heights................................73

Chapter 6:Online Wealth Mindset - Forging Inner Strength for Digital Triumph 75

6.1 Dealing with Failure and Rejection: Learning from the Wilderness........................75

6.2 Overcoming Procrastination and Self-Doubt: Conquering Inner Canaan 78

6.3 Maintaining Work-Life Balance: Embracing the Sabbath of Rest......................................83

6.4 Cultivating Resilience and Persistence: Echoes of Endurance 86

6.5 Celebrating Success: The Importance of Gratitude...89

Forging Inner Strength 91

Chapter 7: Legal and Ethical Considerations - Navigating the Moral Compass of Online Entrepreneurship 92

7.1 Understanding Online Laws and Regulations: A Digital Covenant 92

7.2 Protecting Intellectual Property: Safeguarding Your Digital Inheritance 95

7.3 Maintaining Ethical Standards: Walking in Integrity 99

7.4 Building Trust with Customers and Partners: The Foundation of Covenant 103

7.5 Resolving Disputes and Handling Legal Issues: Wisdom in Resolution 107

Chapter 8: Conclusion - Embarking on Your Digital Odyssey to Online Millions 111

The Digital Promised Land Beckons 111

Embrace the Challenges and Triumphs 112

Unleash Your Potential 112

Your Journey Begins Now 113

Bibliography: 115

Chapter 1: Introduction

Unleashing the Potential of the Digital Frontier

In an era where the digital realm has transformed the way we live, communicate, and do business, the allure of online wealth has captured the imagination of dreamers and entrepreneurs alike. The global connectivity, rapid dissemination of information, and boundless opportunities offered by the online world have turned it into a fertile ground for those seeking financial success and personal fulfillment.

Imagine a landscape where geographical barriers dissolve, where a single idea can reach millions in an instant, and where a venture can flourish without a physical storefront. This is the realm we are delving into – a world where the possibilities are as expansive as the digital horizon itself.

Navigating the Digital Landscape

The digital revolution has democratized the entrepreneurial arena, allowing individuals with determination, creativity, and strategic thinking to unlock unprecedented doors to wealth. Whether you're a visionary entrepreneur with a groundbreaking concept, an artist seeking a global audience, or an expert eager to share your knowledge, the online world provides a platform for your aspirations to take flight.

The Promise of Online Wealth

The promise of making millions online is not a mere illusion. Countless success stories abound – from individuals launching e-commerce empires from their living rooms to creators monetizing their content through digital platforms. The potential for substantial income is real, but it comes with its share of challenges and a need for strategic planning.

A Roadmap to Success

This book is your roadmap to navigating the intricate pathways of online wealth creation. It's not a magic formula for overnight riches, but rather a comprehensive guide that will equip you with the tools, strategies, and insights needed to harness the digital landscape's potential. Each chapter will take you on a journey through the multifaceted aspects of online entrepreneurship – from setting strong foundations to scaling your ventures and cultivating the right mindset.

The Caveats and Considerations

While the online world offers vast opportunities, it also demands adaptability, resilience, and a willingness to learn. Building a successful online enterprise requires more than just technical know-how; it requires a deep understanding of your target audience, dedication to quality, and ethical considerations that build trust.

Embarking on a Transformative Journey

As you embark on this transformative journey through the chapters ahead, remember that success is not a destination but a dynamic process. The online world is ever-evolving, and to thrive, you must embrace change, continually refine your strategies, and stay attuned to emerging trends.

Together, let's unlock the secrets of online wealth and embark on a quest to transform your aspirations into reality. The digital frontier awaits your innovation, your passion, and your dedication to making millions online.

Chapter 2:

Setting the Foundation: Navigating the Digital Frontier of Online Business

2.1 The Evolution of Online Entrepreneurship: A Modern Exodus

The evolution of online entrepreneurship can be likened to the epic journey of the Israelites from captivity to freedom, reflecting a modern exodus. Much like Moses led his people through the wilderness, online entrepreneurs have navigated uncharted territory, forging their own paths in the digital landscape. From the early days of dial-up internet to the current era of lightning-fast connections, this evolution mirrors the journey from constriction to liberation.

In the beginning, online entrepreneurship was a novel concept, with limited technological capabilities and resources. The internet was a new frontier, with entrepreneurs venturing into uncharted territory to carve out their presence in this digital world. Just as the Israelites faced challenges and obstacles on their journey to freedom, online entrepreneurs encountered numerous hurdles and setbacks in their quest for success.

As technology advanced, so did the opportunities for online entrepreneurship. The evolution of the internet brought about faster connections, better communication tools, and a wider reach for businesses to connect with their target audience. This shift in technology mirrored the Israelites' journey through the wilderness, as they encountered new experiences and challenges that shaped their path to liberation.

The rise of social media and e-commerce platforms further revolutionized the landscape of online entrepreneurship. Entrepreneurs now had access to a global audience, allowing them to reach customers from all corners of the world. This expansion of reach and influence mirrored the Israelites' journey towards the promised land, as they traveled far and wide to find their freedom and prosperity.

Just as the Israelites faced moments of doubt and uncertainty on their journey, online entrepreneurs too grappled with challenges and setbacks that tested their resolve. The ever-changing digital landscape required constant adaptation and innovation, forcing entrepreneurs to think creatively and strategically to stay ahead of the curve.

Despite the challenges, online entrepreneurship continued to thrive and evolve, fueled by the relentless drive and determination of those who dared to venture into this new frontier. The journey from captivity to freedom was not an easy one, but it was a journey filled with promise and potential for those who were willing to take the risk and embrace the unknown.

Today, online entrepreneurship has become a thriving industry, with countless success stories that inspire and motivate others to take the leap into this digital world. The evolution of technology has opened up endless possibilities for aspiring entrepreneurs, creating a landscape where anyone with a dream and a vision can turn their ideas into reality.

In conclusion, the evolution of online entrepreneurship mirrors the epic journey of the Israelites from captivity to freedom. Just as Moses led his people through the wilderness, online entrepreneurs have navigated uncharted territory, facing challenges and obstacles along the way. Despite the hardships, the journey towards liberation has been a rewarding one, with opportunities for growth, innovation, and success for those who dared to dream and create their own path in this digital world.

2.2 Identifying Lucrative Online Niches: Finding Your Digital Promised Land

In the vast expanse of the online world, finding your digital promised land can be a daunting task. With millions of websites and businesses vying for attention, standing out and making a mark can seem like an insurmountable challenge. However, just as the Promised Land was a place of abundance and opportunity for the Israelites, there are lucrative online niches waiting to be discovered by savvy entrepreneurs.

Like Abraham being led by God to a land flowing with milk and honey, your journey to finding a profitable online niche requires guidance and direction. This starts with thorough research and insight into the needs and desires of your target audience. By understanding their pain points, desires, and preferences, you can tailor your products or services to meet their needs effectively. This is the first step towards building a successful online business that resonates with your audience and drives profitability.

But how do you go about finding your digital promised land? The key lies in identifying niche markets that are underserved or overlooked by larger businesses. These niches may not have the same level of competition as more mainstream industries, making it easier for you to establish yourself as a leader in that space. Additionally, these niches may have a dedicated and passionate customer base willing to pay a premium for products or services that meet their specific needs.

To start your search for a lucrative online niche, consider your own interests, skills, and expertise. What are you passionate about? What are you good at? By aligning your business with your interests and strengths, you are more likely to enjoy the work you do and create a business that resonates with your values and vision. This will also set you apart from competitors who may lack the same level of personal connection to their niche.

Next, research potential niches to identify those with high growth potential and low competition. Use tools like Google Trends, keyword research tools, and social media analytics to uncover trends and opportunities in different industries. Look for niches with a large and engaged audience, as well as products or services that are in high demand but not readily available.

Once you have identified a few potential niches, delve deeper into market research to understand the needs and preferences of your target audience. Conduct surveys, interviews, and focus groups to gather valuable insights into what your customers are looking for in a product or service. Use this data to refine your business idea and tailor your offerings to meet the specific needs of your target market.

In addition to understanding your audience, it is essential to assess the competitive landscape of your chosen niche. Who are your main competitors? What are their strengths and weaknesses? How can you differentiate your business from theirs and carve out a unique position in the market? By conducting a competitive analysis, you can identify gaps in the market that you can fill with your own offerings.

Another key factor in finding your digital promised land is considering the profitability and scalability of your chosen niche. Will you be able to generate a healthy profit margin from your products or services? Is there room for growth and expansion in the market? By evaluating the financial viability of your niche, you can ensure that your business has the potential for long-term success and sustainability.

Once you have identified a lucrative online niche that aligns with your interests, skills, and expertise, it is time to develop a comprehensive business plan. This plan should outline your goals, strategies, and tactics for reaching your target audience and driving profitability. It should also include a detailed marketing strategy to promote your products or services and attract customers to your business.

In conclusion, finding your digital promised land is a journey that requires patience, perseverance, and strategic thinking. By conducting thorough research, understanding your target audience, and evaluating the competition and profitability of your chosen niche, you can position yourself for success in the online world. Just as God guided Abraham to a land of abundance, meticulous planning and insight will lead you to your online haven of prosperity. With the right strategy and determination, you can build a thriving online business that fulfills your entrepreneurial dreams and provides value to your customers.

2.3 The Importance of Keyword Research: Digital Stones of Success

Keyword research is often seen as the backbone of successful online visibility. Just as David carefully selected the stones he used to defeat Goliath, businesses must also choose their keywords wisely in order to reach their target audience effectively. In the world of digital marketing, keywords serve as the cornerstone of any successful SEO strategy, helping businesses to connect with their desired customers and drive traffic to their websites.

Much like David's stone found its mark and struck Goliath down, the right keywords can help businesses to capture the attention of their target audience and stand out in a crowded online marketplace. Through careful research and analysis, businesses can identify the keywords that are most relevant to their products or services, and use them strategically to boost their search engine rankings and attract more organic traffic.

Keyword research is not just about selecting a few random words and hoping for the best. It requires a deep understanding of your target audience, your industry, and your competition. By identifying the keywords that are most commonly used by your target customers when searching for products or services like yours, you can tailor your content to meet their needs and preferences, and improve your chances of being found online.

Just as David's skillful aim with his stones allowed him to overcome Goliath's size and strength, businesses that excel at keyword research can outperform their competitors and achieve greater visibility in the digital landscape. By incorporating the right keywords into their website content, blog posts, and other marketing materials, businesses can increase their chances of ranking well in search engine results and attracting more qualified leads to their websites.

In essence, keyword research is the secret weapon that can help businesses to achieve digital success. By uncovering the words and phrases that are most relevant to their target audience and incorporating them strategically into their online content, businesses can improve their search engine rankings, drive more traffic to their websites, and ultimately, increase their sales and revenue.

Just as David's strategic use of his stones enabled him to defeat Goliath and emerge victorious, businesses that prioritize keyword research in their digital marketing efforts can overcome the challenges of the online landscape and achieve success in today's competitive marketplace. By investing time and resources into researching and selecting the right keywords for their business, companies can set themselves up for long-term success and ensure that their online presence is strong, resilient, and effective at reaching their target audience.

In conclusion, keyword research is the cornerstone of any successful digital marketing strategy. By carefully selecting and using the right keywords in their online content, businesses can improve their visibility, attract more organic traffic, and ultimately achieve their goals of driving sales and revenue. Just as David's well-aimed stones were instrumental in his victory over Goliath, businesses that excel at keyword research can overcome the challenges of the digital landscape and emerge as leaders in their industry.

Crafting Your Online Path

As you journey through the foundation of online business, remember that just as the Israelites faced trials and triumphs in their pursuit of the Promised Land, your path will be marked by challenges and victories. The evolution of online entrepreneurship, the search for lucrative niches, and the power of keywords are the cornerstones of your digital odyssey. Let the wisdom of scripture guide you as you navigate this modern landscape, armed with insights from the past to shape your prosperous future.

Chapter 3:

Building Your Online Empire Forging Essential Strategies in the Digital Realm

3.1 Creating a Strong Online Presence: Your Digital Pillar of Cloud and Fire

Creating a strong online presence is crucial for any business in today's digital age. Just like the pillar of cloud and fire guided the Israelites, your online presence serves as a beacon that leads your audience towards your brand. It is a reflection of who you are, what you stand for, and what you have to offer. In essence, your online presence becomes your digital pillar of cloud and fire, guiding and illuminating the way for your target audience to find and engage with your brand.

When it comes to establishing a strong online presence, there are several key components that need to be considered. These include having a well-designed website, engaging social media presence, and consistent branding across all platforms. Your website is often the first point of contact for potential customers, so it's essential that it is visually appealing, user-friendly, and provides valuable information about your products or services. Think of your website as the foundation of your digital presence, the pillar on which everything else is built upon.

In addition to having a strong website, a presence on social media is also essential for connecting with your audience and reaching a wider customer base. Social media platforms such as Facebook, Instagram, Twitter, and LinkedIn provide opportunities to engage with your audience in real-time, share updates and promotions, and build relationships with potential customers. By creating a consistent presence on these platforms, you can establish credibility and trust with your audience, much like the pillar of cloud and fire guided the Israelites through the wilderness.

Another important aspect of creating a strong online presence is maintaining consistent branding across all platforms. Your brand identity is what sets you apart from your competitors and helps to create a cohesive and recognizable image for your business. From your logo and color scheme to your tone of voice and messaging, consistency is key in building a strong and memorable brand presence online. Just as the pillar of cloud and fire was a symbol of God's presence and guidance for the Israelites, your branding should be a symbol of your business's values and offerings for your audience.

Furthermore, creating quality content is essential for building a strong online presence. Whether it's blog posts, videos, infographics, or social media updates, consistently creating and sharing valuable content helps to establish your authority in your industry and attract and engage your target audience. By providing content that is informative, entertaining, and relevant to your audience's needs and interests, you can build trust and credibility with your followers and keep them coming back for more.

In addition to creating quality content, engaging with your audience is also key to building a strong online presence. Responding to comments and messages, participating in conversations, and soliciting feedback from your audience shows that you care about their opinions and values their input. By establishing a two-way dialogue with your audience, you can build a loyal following that will advocate for your brand and help spread the word about your products or services.

Lastly, monitoring and analyzing your online presence is essential for measuring the effectiveness of your efforts and making informed decisions about your digital marketing strategy. By tracking key metrics such as website traffic, social media engagement, and conversion rates, you can identify what is working well and what can be improved upon. By using tools such as Google Analytics, social media insights, and customer feedback surveys, you can gain valuable insights into your audience's behavior and preferences, allowing you to tailor your online presence to better meet their needs.

In conclusion, creating a strong online presence is essential for any business looking to thrive in today's digital landscape. By establishing a well-designed website, engaging social media presence, consistent branding, quality content, and active engagement with your audience, you can build a digital pillar of cloud and fire that illuminates the way for your target audience to find and connect with your brand. Just as the pillar of cloud and fire guided the Israelites through the wilderness, your online presence can serve as a beacon that leads your audience towards your brand and helps you stand out in a crowded marketplace.

3.2 Developing a Profitable Website or Blog: Crafting Your Online Ark

Crafting a profitable website or blog is no easy task. It requires careful planning, attention to detail, and a clear understanding of your audience's needs. Just as Noah meticulously constructed his ark to provide refuge from the flood, you must create a platform that serves as a sanctuary for your ideas, products, and services.

To begin, you must have a clear purpose for your website or blog. What are you hoping to achieve with this platform? Are you looking to sell products or services, share valuable information, or build a community of like-minded individuals? By defining your goals upfront, you can ensure that every aspect of your website or blog is aligned with your objectives.

Next, you must consider the design and layout of your website or blog. Just as Noah carefully planned the dimensions and compartments of his ark, you must think about how to structure your platform in a way that is user-friendly and visually appealing. This includes choosing a clean and professional design, organizing your content in a logical manner, and optimizing for mobile devices.

In addition to the design, you must also focus on creating high-quality content. Just as Noah brought pairs of every animal onto his ark, you must populate your website or blog with valuable information that will attract and engage your audience. This may include blog posts, articles, videos, podcasts, or other forms of content that are relevant to your target market.

It's also important to regularly update your website or blog with fresh content. Just as Noah had to care for the animals on his ark, you must nurture your platform by consistently producing new material that keeps your audience coming back for more. This not only helps to improve your search engine rankings but also demonstrates your commitment to providing value to your readers.

Furthermore, you must consider how to monetize your website or blog. Just as Noah had to ensure that his ark was sustainable for the long term, you must find ways to generate revenue from your platform. This could include selling products or services, displaying ads, affiliate marketing, sponsored content, or other monetization strategies that align with your goals and audience.

Finally, you must focus on driving traffic to your website or blog. Just as Noah needed to attract animals to his ark, you must find ways to attract visitors to your platform. This may involve implementing search engine optimization (SEO) techniques, promoting your content on social media, collaborating with other bloggers or websites, or running advertising campaigns.

In conclusion, crafting a profitable website or blog is a meticulous process that requires careful planning, attention to detail, and a clear purpose. By following the steps outlined above, you can create a platform that serves as a sanctuary for your ideas, products, and services, and ultimately, achieve success in the online world. Just as Noah's ark provided refuge from the flood, your website or blog can provide refuge for your audience's needs.

3.3 Leveraging Social Media for Maximum Impact: The New Digital Marketplace

In today's digital age, social media has become an essential tool for businesses looking to maximize their impact in the marketplace. Just as merchants in bustling marketplaces of old gathered to showcase their wares, businesses now congregate on social media platforms to connect with potential customers on a global scale.

Social media serves as a virtual marketplace, providing businesses with a platform to promote their products and services, engage with customers, and build brand awareness. With billions of users worldwide, platforms such as Facebook, Instagram, Twitter, and LinkedIn offer businesses the opportunity to reach a vast audience with just the click of a button.

One of the key benefits of leveraging social media for marketing purposes is the ability to engage in real-time conversations with customers. Just as the marketplace was a hub of interaction, social media facilitates two-way communication between businesses and consumers. This allows businesses to gather valuable feedback, address customer concerns, and provide timely updates on products and services.

In addition to facilitating conversation, social media also allows businesses to showcase their personalities and values. By sharing engaging content, businesses can humanize their brand and connect with customers on a more personal level. This can help build trust and loyalty among customers, leading to increased brand awareness and customer retention.

Another advantage of using social media for marketing is the ability to target specific demographics. With advanced targeting options available on platforms like Facebook and Instagram, businesses can tailor their marketing efforts to reach their ideal customers. This level of precision targeting can help businesses maximize their marketing budget and increase their return on investment.

Furthermore, social media provides businesses with valuable data and analytics to measure the success of their marketing campaigns. By tracking metrics such as engagement rates, click-through rates, and conversion rates, businesses can gain insight into the effectiveness of their social media efforts and make data-driven decisions to optimize their strategies.

In order to maximize the impact of social media marketing, businesses should focus on creating high-quality, engaging content that resonates with their target audience. This can include a mix of visual content, such as images and videos, as well as written content, such as blog posts and articles. By consistently posting valuable content, businesses can attract and retain followers, ultimately driving traffic and conversions.

Additionally, businesses should be proactive in engaging with their audience by responding to comments, messages, and reviews in a timely manner. This can help build trust and credibility with customers, as well as foster a sense of community around the brand. By fostering positive relationships with customers on social media, businesses can create brand advocates who will help promote their products and services to their own networks.

In conclusion, social media presents businesses with a valuable opportunity to maximize their impact in the digital marketplace. By leveraging social media platforms to promote their products and services, engage with customers, and build brand awareness, businesses can reach a global audience and drive growth for their business. Through strategic content creation, targeted advertising, and proactive engagement, businesses can harness the power of social media to achieve their marketing goals and stay ahead of the competition in today's fast-paced digital world.

3.4 Email Marketing: The Key to Long-Term Success

Email marketing has become the cornerstone of successful digital marketing strategies for businesses around the world. Just like how Abraham's covenant with God was a foundation for generations, email marketing serves as a modern covenant between businesses and their audience. It provides a platform for businesses to offer valuable content, build trust, and establish lasting connections over time.

Email marketing is not just a one-time promotional tool, but rather a long-term strategy that promises continued engagement and growth. It allows businesses to stay connected with their audience, provide them with relevant content, and keep them informed about new products or services. Just as Abraham's covenant was a promise of prosperity, email marketing promises business growth and success.

One of the key advantages of email marketing is its ability to reach a wide audience in a cost-effective manner. With just a click of a button, businesses can send out personalized messages to thousands of subscribers, making it an efficient way to communicate with customers and prospects. This targeted approach helps businesses build relationships with their audience, leading to increased brand loyalty and customer retention.

Another benefit of email marketing is its trackability and measurability. Businesses can track metrics such as open rates, click-through rates, and conversion rates to gauge the effectiveness of their email campaigns. This data can be used to optimize future campaigns, improve engagement rates, and ultimately drive more sales.

Furthermore, email marketing allows businesses to deliver personalized content to their audience based on their preferences and interests. By segmenting their email list and sending targeted messages, businesses can ensure that their subscribers receive content that is relevant and valuable to them. This personalized approach helps businesses build trust with their audience and establish themselves as experts in their industry.

In addition, email marketing is a versatile tool that can be used for a variety of purposes. Businesses can use email to promote new products or services, announce upcoming events, share company news, or even provide educational content to their audience. By diversifying their email content, businesses can keep their subscribers engaged and interested in what they have to offer.

Overall, email marketing is a powerful tool that can help businesses build lasting connections with their audience and drive long-term success. Just like how Abraham's covenant stood the test of time, email marketing can serve as a foundation for businesses to grow and prosper for generations to come. By providing valuable content, forging trust, and delivering personalized messages, businesses can leverage the power of email marketing to cultivate strong relationships with their audience and achieve their business goals. Email marketing truly is the key to long-term success.

3.5 Effective Search Engine Optimization (SEO) Techniques: Navigating the Digital Wilderness

In today's digital landscape, having effective search engine optimization (SEO) techniques is crucial for the success of your content. Just as the Israelites relied on guidance to navigate the wilderness, your content needs proper SEO strategies to be found by those seeking it. Without the right SEO techniques, your content may get lost in the vast digital wilderness, hindering its visibility and reach.

One of the most important SEO techniques is keyword optimization. Keywords are the words or phrases that people use to search for information online. By strategically incorporating relevant keywords into your content, you can increase the likelihood of your content appearing in search engine results pages (SERPs). Conducting keyword research to identify the most relevant and valuable keywords for your content is essential for effective SEO. Consider factors such as search volume, competition, and user intent when selecting keywords to optimize your content.

Another crucial SEO technique is creating high-quality, engaging content. Search engines like Google prioritize content that is valuable, informative, and engaging for users. By creating content that is relevant to your audience and addresses their needs and interests, you can attract more organic traffic to your website. Incorporate multimedia elements such as images, videos, and infographics to make your content more visually appealing and increase user engagement.

In addition to keyword optimization and high-quality content creation, link building is another important SEO technique to consider. Search engines view links as signals of trust and authority. By building high-quality backlinks from reputable and relevant websites, you can improve your website's credibility and visibility in search results. Focus on acquiring backlinks from websites with high domain authority and relevancy to your content to maximize the impact of your link-building efforts.

Optimizing your website's technical aspects is also crucial for effective SEO. Ensure that your website is mobile-friendly, loads quickly, and is easy to navigate for users. Search engines prioritize websites that provide a seamless user experience, so optimizing your site's technical aspects can help improve your search engine rankings. Additionally, consider implementing structured data markup to help search engines understand your content better and potentially enhance your website's visibility in SERPs.

Monitoring and analyzing your SEO performance is essential for identifying areas for improvement and optimizing your strategies. Use tools like Google Analytics and Google Search Console to track your website's performance, analyze key metrics, and identify opportunities for optimization. Regularly review your keyword rankings, organic traffic, and conversion rates to gauge the effectiveness of your SEO efforts and make data-driven decisions to enhance your online presence.

In conclusion, effective search engine optimization techniques are essential for navigating the digital wilderness and ensuring that your content is discovered by those seeking it. By implementing strategies such as keyword optimization, high-quality content creation, link building, and technical optimization, you can improve your website's visibility, attract more organic traffic, and ultimately drive better results for your online presence. Stay proactive in monitoring and analyzing your SEO performance, and continuously adapt and optimize your strategies to stay ahead in the competitive digital landscape.

Pillars of Your Online Empire

In this chapter, you'll lay the pillars of your online empire. Creating a strong presence, building a profitable website, leveraging social media, mastering email marketing, and implementing effective SEO techniques are the foundational elements that will shape your digital legacy. Just as the Israelites built an enduring nation, these strategies will enable you to construct a thriving online presence.

Chapter 4:

Monetizing Your Online Ventures - Forging Diverse Pathways to Financial Abundance

4.1 Affiliate Marketing: Earning Commissions

Affiliate marketing is a widely popular and effective way for individuals to earn commissions by promoting products or services created by others. It is essentially a performance-based marketing strategy where affiliates receive a commission for each sale or lead they generate for the merchant.

The concept of affiliate marketing can be likened to the Biblical story of Joseph, who used his foresight to save Egypt from famine by wisely managing resources. In a similar way, affiliates can use their skills and knowledge to strategically promote products or services to their audience and earn commissions in return.

One of the key principles of affiliate marketing is selecting the right affiliates to work with. Just as Joseph carefully chose how to distribute resources in order to maximize their impact, affiliates must also choose products or services that align with their values and beliefs. By promoting products they genuinely believe in, affiliates can build trust with their audience and establish themselves as a reliable source of information.

Affiliate marketing offers a win-win scenario for both affiliates and merchants. Affiliates have the opportunity to earn commissions by promoting products or services they believe in, while merchants benefit from increased visibility and sales. This mutually beneficial relationship is similar to Joseph's wise management of resources, where both parties benefit from working together towards a common goal.

In order to be successful in affiliate marketing, affiliates must be strategic in their approach. It is important to carefully select products or services that are relevant to their audience and align with their niche. By understanding their audience's needs and preferences, affiliates can create targeted campaigns that resonate with their audience and drive conversions.

Just as Joseph's foresight allowed him to prepare for the famine and save Egypt from disaster, affiliates must also have a vision for the future and adapt to changing market trends. By continuously monitoring their campaigns and analyzing data, affiliates can optimize their strategies and maximize their earning potential.

In conclusion, affiliate marketing offers a unique opportunity for individuals to earn commissions by promoting products or services created by others. By selecting the right affiliates, promoting products they believe in, and being strategic in their approach, affiliates can build a successful affiliate marketing business and earn commissions while benefiting their audience. Like Joseph's wise management of resources, affiliate marketing requires careful planning and foresight to reap a bountiful harvest.

4.2 Selling Digital Products: Crafting and Selling Your Digital Artifacts

Crafting and selling digital products has become a lucrative opportunity for creatives and experts in various fields. In today's digital world, there are endless possibilities for sharing your expertise with a global audience. Just like Bezalel, who crafted the intricate items for the Tabernacle, creating digital artifacts allows you to showcase your skills and knowledge in a unique and valuable way.

One of the most popular digital products is an e-book. E-books are a great way to share in-depth knowledge on a specific topic with readers who are eager to learn. Whether you are an expert in a certain niche or have valuable insights to offer, writing an e-book can be a rewarding experience. With the rise of e-readers and digital platforms, selling e-books has become easier than ever before. You can self-publish your e-book on platforms like

Amazon Kindle Direct Publishing or sell it through your own website.

Another popular digital product is an online course. Online courses have become increasingly popular as more people seek to enhance their skills and knowledge from the comfort of their own homes. As an expert in your field, you can create an online course that delivers valuable content in a structured and engaging way. Platforms like Teachable, Udemy, and Skillshare make it easy to create and sell online courses to a global audience. By sharing your expertise through an online course, you can help others learn and grow in their chosen field.

In addition to e-books and online courses, there are many other types of digital products you can create and sell. This includes templates, toolkits, audio guides, video tutorials, and more. The key is to identify your unique expertise and find a digital product that will resonate with your target audience. By creating valuable and high-quality digital products, you can establish yourself as a thought leader in your field and generate passive income streams.

When it comes to selling digital products, it's important to have a strategic marketing plan in place. This includes identifying your target audience, creating a compelling sales page, and promoting your products through social media, email marketing, and other channels. It's also important to consider pricing strategies, such as offering discounts or bundling products together to increase sales.

Overall, crafting and selling digital products is a rewarding way to share your expertise with the world and generate income from your skills and knowledge. Whether you choose to create e-books, online courses, or other digital artifacts, the possibilities are endless. By leveraging digital platforms and marketing strategies, you can reach a global audience and make a meaningful impact with your creations. Just like Bezalel's craftsmanship in the Tabernacle, your digital creations have the power to inspire, educate, and enrich the lives of others.

4.3 Dropshipping: Curating an E-commerce Store without Inventory

Dropshipping has revolutionized the e-commerce industry, allowing entrepreneurs to curate online stores without the need for storing inventory. Much like the Israelites' efficient management of their desert supplies, dropshipping offers a streamlined and cost-effective way to run a business.

In a dropshipping business model, the entrepreneur partners with suppliers who hold the inventory and handle the shipping of products directly to customers. This eliminates the need for the business owner to have a physical storage space for their goods, saving on costs associated with warehousing and inventory management.

Just as God provided manna daily to the Israelites in the desert, dropshipping ensures that products reach customers in a timely manner without the excess storage requirements. By leveraging partnerships with suppliers, entrepreneurs can offer a wide range of products on their e-commerce store without the overhead costs of maintaining inventory.

One of the key benefits of dropshipping is the ability to quickly and easily scale your business. Without the constraints of physical inventory, entrepreneurs can easily add new products to their store and test out different markets without the risk of excess stock. This flexibility allows for rapid growth and adaptability in response to changing consumer demands.

Additionally, dropshipping offers a low barrier to entry for aspiring entrepreneurs. With minimal startup costs and no need for a physical storefront, anyone can launch an e-commerce store and start selling products online. This accessibility has democratized the world of retail, allowing individuals from all backgrounds to start and grow their own businesses.

In a traditional retail model, the entrepreneur must invest in inventory upfront, taking on the risk of holding onto unsold stock. However, with dropshipping, this risk is transferred to the supplier, who only ships products once they have been ordered by customers. This "just-in-time" approach to inventory management minimizes the risk of overstocking and reduces the financial burden on the business owner.

Furthermore, dropshipping allows entrepreneurs to focus on what they do best – marketing and customer service. By outsourcing the logistics of inventory management and shipping to suppliers, entrepreneurs can devote more time and resources to growing their business and providing exceptional service to their customers. This specialization leads to increased efficiency and effectiveness in running an e-commerce store.

The success of a dropshipping business ultimately hinges on the quality of the supplier relationships. It is crucial to partner with reliable and trustworthy suppliers who can fulfill orders quickly and accurately. Establishing strong communication channels and setting clear expectations with suppliers is key to maintaining a smooth operation and ensuring customer satisfaction.

In conclusion, dropshipping is a game-changer for e-commerce entrepreneurs looking to build a successful online store without the burden of storing inventory. By leveraging partnerships with suppliers, entrepreneurs can offer a wide range of products to customers while focusing on marketing and customer service. With its low barrier to entry and scalability, dropshipping is a versatile and cost-effective business model that empowers anyone to start and grow their own e-commerce business. Just as the Israelites efficiently managed their desert supplies, dropshipping allows entrepreneurs to thrive in the competitive world of online retail.

4.4 Online Advertising: Maximizing Revenue through Digital Billboards

In today's digital age, online advertising has become essential for businesses looking to reach a wider audience and increase their revenue. Just like the banners that were used in ancient times to announce the goods and services of merchants, digital billboards serve as a modern-day equivalent to attract potential customers to your offerings. Much like the riches of King Solomon, which drew visitors from distant lands, your digital billboards have the power to attract audiences from all over the world to your products and services.

One of the key factors in maximizing revenue through online advertising is optimizing ad placements and targeting. Ad placements refer to where your ads are displayed on websites, social media platforms, search engines, and other online channels. By strategically placing your ads in areas where your target audience is most likely to see them, you can increase the chances of them clicking on the ad and making a purchase.

Targeting, on the other hand, involves identifying and reaching out to specific groups of people who are most likely to be interested in your products or services. This can be done through demographic information such as age, gender, location, interests, and behavior. By targeting your ads towards these specific groups, you can increase the effectiveness of your advertising campaigns and ultimately maximize your revenue.

There are various ways to optimize ad placements and targeting in online advertising. One way is through the use of data analytics and artificial intelligence. By analyzing data on user behavior, interests, and preferences, you can determine the best placements for your ads and the most effective targeting strategies. Artificial intelligence can also help automate the process of optimizing ad placements and targeting, saving you time and resources while improving the performance of your campaigns.

Another way to maximize revenue through online advertising is by utilizing retargeting strategies. Retargeting allows you to reach out to users who have previously interacted with your ads or visited your website but did not make a purchase. By showing these users targeted ads based on their past interactions, you can encourage them to revisit your website and make a purchase. Retargeting has been shown to be highly effective in increasing conversion rates and driving revenue for businesses.

In addition to optimizing ad placements, targeting, and retargeting strategies, it is also important to continuously monitor and analyze the performance of your online advertising campaigns. By tracking key metrics such as click-through rates, conversion rates, and return on investment, you can identify areas for improvement and make data-driven decisions to maximize your revenue.

Furthermore, it is important to stay updated on the latest trends and technologies in online advertising. As the digital landscape continues to evolve, new opportunities and challenges arise for businesses looking to maximize their revenue through digital billboards and other forms of online advertising. By staying informed and adapting to changes in the industry, you can stay ahead of the competition and continue to drive revenue through your online advertising efforts.

In conclusion, online advertising is a powerful tool for businesses looking to maximize their revenue and reach a wider audience. By optimizing ad placements, targeting, retargeting strategies, and monitoring campaign performance, you can effectively promote your products and services to potential customers and drive revenue for your business. With the right strategies and tools in place, your digital billboards have the potential to attract audiences from all over the world and increase your revenue significantly.

4.5 Freelancing and Consulting: Sharing Your Expertise

Freelancing and consulting are two incredibly valuable ways to share your expertise and make a living. Just like Moses served as a guide and a source of wisdom for the Israelites, freelancing and consulting allow you to offer your knowledge and skills to those in need of guidance. Through these avenues, you can lead clients towards their goals, generate income, and foster personal and professional growth.

When it comes to freelancing, you have the freedom to work on your terms and take on projects that align with your expertise and interests. Whether you're a writer, graphic designer, web developer, or consultant in a specific field, freelancing allows you to showcase your talents and make a name for yourself in your industry. By working with a variety of clients, you can gain valuable experience, expand your network, and build a portfolio that highlights your skills and accomplishments.

One of the key benefits of freelancing is the flexibility it offers. You have the freedom to choose your own hours, set your own rates, and work from anywhere in the world. This flexibility allows you to balance work and personal life, pursue other interests, and take on multiple projects at once. As a freelancer, you have the autonomy to pick and choose the projects that interest you and align with your values, giving you a sense of fulfillment and satisfaction in your work.

Consulting, on the other hand, involves providing expert advice and guidance to individuals, businesses, or organizations in a specific field. As a consultant, your role is to analyze problems, offer solutions, and help clients achieve their goals. Whether you specialize in marketing, finance, HR, or another area, consulting allows you to leverage your expertise and help others succeed.

Consulting is a highly lucrative and rewarding career path for those with specialized knowledge and skills. By providing valuable insights and recommendations, consultants can help clients improve their operations, increase efficiency, and drive growth. Whether you work independently or for a consulting firm, you have the opportunity to make a significant impact on your clients' success and contribute to their long-term growth and sustainability.

In both freelancing and consulting, communication and relationship-building are key to success. As a freelancer or consultant, you must be able to effectively communicate with clients, understand their needs, and provide solutions that meet their goals. Building strong relationships with clients is essential for gaining their trust and loyalty, as well as for securing repeat business and referrals.

Additionally, freelancers and consultants must stay current with industry trends, technologies, and best practices to remain competitive and relevant in their field. Continuing education, attending conferences, and networking with other professionals are all important for expanding your knowledge and skills and staying ahead of the curve.

While freelancing and consulting offer many opportunities for personal and professional growth, they also come with their own set of challenges. As a freelancer, you may struggle with finding a consistent stream of clients, managing your time effectively, and setting boundaries between work and personal life. As a consultant, you may face difficulties in building credibility, establishing your reputation, and differentiating yourself from competitors.

Despite these challenges, freelancing and consulting can be incredibly rewarding for those who are passionate about sharing their expertise and helping others succeed. By leveraging your knowledge and skills, you have the power to make a positive impact on clients' lives and businesses and contribute to their growth and success. Whether you're guiding clients towards their goals, offering solutions to their problems, or providing insights and advice, freelancing and consulting allow you to make a difference in the world while generating income and pursuing your passion.

Personal Testimony: Navigating the Digital Oasis

As I embarked on my own online journey, these monetization strategies became my oasis in the digital desert. Through affiliate marketing, I've not only earned commissions but also built a network of trusted partners. Creating and selling digital products allowed me to share my passion while generating income. The dropshipping model provided me the freedom to operate an e-commerce venture without the burden of inventory. Online advertising brought visibility to my offerings, while freelancing and consulting empowered me to share my expertise with those seeking guidance. Just as the Israelites journeyed through the wilderness, each strategy has been a stepping stone toward financial abundance in the digital realm.

Pillars of Prosperity

In this chapter, we've laid down the pillars of diverse income streams. Just as the Israelites cultivated the land, these strategies allow you to cultivate your online ventures. From affiliate marketing to freelancing, you have an array of tools to transform your online presence into a realm of financial prosperity. Just as the Israelites reaped the rewards of their efforts, these strategies can yield bountiful results for you.

Chapter 5:

Scaling Your Online Business - Ascending to New Heights in the Digital Horizon

5.1 Outsourcing and Automation: Streamlining Operations

Outsourcing and automation have become indispensable tools for businesses looking to streamline their operations in today's fast-paced world. By delegating tasks to skilled professionals and leveraging technology, companies can focus on their core competencies and drive growth and efficiency. Just like Jethro advised Moses to delegate responsibilities, modern businesses can benefit from a strategic approach to outsourcing and automation.

Outsourcing has been a common practice for companies looking to lower costs, access specialized skills, and increase operational efficiency. By partnering with third-party service providers, businesses can delegate non-core tasks such as IT services, accounting, customer support, and manufacturing, allowing them to focus on their core competencies. This not only reduces costs by avoiding the need to hire and train in-house staff but also provides access to specialized expertise that can drive innovation and growth.

Automation, on the other hand, involves using technology to streamline repetitive tasks and processes, reducing the need for human intervention and increasing efficiency. From robotic process automation (RPA) to artificial intelligence (AI) and machine learning, businesses can automate a wide range of tasks, such as data entry, inventory management, customer service, and even decision-making processes. This not only saves time and resources but also reduces the risk of errors and improves accuracy and consistency.

By combining outsourcing and automation, businesses can create a seamless and efficient operational ecosystem that allows them to focus on strategic activities and drive growth. For example, a manufacturing company can outsource its supply chain management to a third-party logistics provider while automating inventory management and production scheduling, resulting in lower costs, faster delivery times, and improved customer satisfaction.

Outsourcing and automation can also help businesses adapt to changing market conditions and stay competitive in today's digital economy. For example, an e-commerce company can outsource its digital marketing efforts to a specialized agency while using AI-powered tools to personalize customer recommendations and automate order fulfillment processes. This not only improves the customer experience but also allows the company to scale its operations and expand into new markets.

However, outsourcing and automation are not without their challenges. Businesses need to carefully assess their outsourcing needs, select the right partners, and establish clear communication channels to ensure the success of their outsourcing initiatives. Similarly, implementing automation technologies requires careful planning, testing, and monitoring to prevent disruptions and ensure the desired outcomes.

Overall, outsourcing and automation are powerful tools that can help businesses streamline their operations, drive growth, and stay competitive in today's fast-paced world. By delegating tasks to skilled professionals and leveraging technology, companies can focus on their core competencies and achieve operational excellence. Just as Jethro advised Moses to delegate responsibilities, modern businesses can benefit from a strategic approach to outsourcing and automation in order to thrive in the digital age.

5.2 Expanding Your Reach: Targeting International Markets

Expanding your reach to target international markets is an exciting opportunity for your online business. Just as God's blessings transcend borders, your products and services have the potential to reach a global audience. In the same way that the Magi journeyed to see Jesus, customers from around the world are eager to explore what you have to offer.

Expanding into international markets can bring a whole new level of growth and success to your business. With the right strategies in place, you can bridge cultural gaps and connect with diverse audiences in a meaningful way. In this section, we will explore the steps you can take to expand your reach and effectively target international markets.

1. Conduct Market Research

Before expanding into international markets, it is essential to conduct thorough market research. This will help you understand the needs, preferences, and behaviors of your target audience in different countries. You will also need to research the competitive landscape in each market to identify opportunities and challenges.

By gaining a deep understanding of the international markets you are targeting, you can tailor your marketing strategies and product offerings to meet the specific needs of customers in each region. This will increase your chances of success and help you stand out from the competition.

2. Develop a Multilingual Website

One of the most important steps in expanding to international markets is to create a multilingual website. This will allow customers from different countries to easily access your products and services in their native language. A multilingual website shows that you value and respect the cultural diversity of your global audience, which can help build trust and credibility.

When translating your website content, make sure to use professional translators who are fluent in the target language. This will ensure that your message is accurately conveyed and resonates with your international customers. You may also need to consider localizing your website to adapt to cultural differences and preferences in each market.

3. Localize Your Marketing Strategies

In addition to a multilingual website, it is important to localize your marketing strategies for each international market. This includes tailoring your advertising campaigns, social media content, and email marketing messages to resonate with the cultural norms and preferences of customers in different countries.

By understanding the cultural nuances of your target audience, you can create more relevant and engaging marketing content that drives customer engagement and loyalty. This personalized approach will show customers that you care about their specific needs and values, which can lead to increased sales and brand loyalty.

4. Partner with Local Distributors or Agents

To successfully penetrate international markets, you may need to partner with local distributors or agents who have a strong understanding of the local market dynamics and customer preferences. These partners can help you navigate the complexities of doing business in a foreign country and provide valuable insights into the best strategies for success.

By collaborating with local partners, you can leverage their expertise and networks to expand your reach and increase your market penetration. This can help you establish a strong presence in international markets and build long-lasting relationships with customers around the world.

5. Provide Excellent Customer Support

As you expand into international markets, it is crucial to provide excellent customer support to meet the unique needs of customers in different countries. This includes offering multilingual customer service, providing clear information on shipping and returns policies, and responding promptly to customer inquiries and feedback.

By delivering exceptional customer support, you can build trust and loyalty with your international customers, which can lead to repeat business and positive word-of-mouth recommendations. This will help you establish a strong reputation in international markets and differentiate yourself from competitors.

In conclusion, expanding your reach to target international markets is a rewarding and challenging journey for your online business. By conducting thorough market research, developing a multilingual website, localizing your marketing strategies, partnering with local distributors, and providing excellent customer support, you can successfully connect with diverse audiences around the world and achieve long-term success and growth. Just as the Magi journeyed to see Jesus, your global customers are eager to explore what you have to offer – so seize the opportunity and expand your horizons today!

5.3 Building a Brand: Establishing Trust and Credibility

Building a brand is not an easy task; it requires dedication, hard work, and a deep understanding of your audience. Just like the Israelites trusted Moses to lead them to the promised land, your audience must trust your brand to deliver on its promises and provide value. In order to establish trust and credibility, it is essential to prioritize consistency, authenticity, and delivering value in all aspects of your brand.

Consistency is key when it comes to building a brand that resonates with your audience. This means that your brand message, voice, and visual identity should remain consistent across all channels and touchpoints. Whether it's your website, social media, or marketing materials, your audience should be able to easily recognize your brand and understand what you stand for. Consistency helps to build familiarity and trust with your audience, as they come to rely on your brand to consistently deliver on its promises.

Authenticity is another crucial component of building a brand that establishes trust and credibility. Your audience wants to connect with a brand that is genuine, transparent, and real. This means staying true to your values, beliefs, and mission, even when faced with challenges or difficult decisions. Authenticity builds trust with your audience, as they can see that you are genuine in your intentions and actions. Authenticity also helps to differentiate your brand from competitors, as it allows you to showcase what makes your brand unique and special.

Delivering value is perhaps the most important aspect of building a brand that resonates with your audience. Your audience should see your brand as a valuable resource that meets their needs, solves their problems, and enriches their lives in some way. Whether it's through your products, services, content, or customer interactions, your brand should consistently provide value to your audience. By delivering value, you not only build trust and credibility with your audience, but you also create loyal customers who are willing to advocate for your brand and spread the word to others.

In order to build a brand that establishes trust and credibility, it is important to focus on these three key elements: consistency, authenticity, and delivering value. By prioritizing these aspects in all aspects of your brand, you can create a legacy that stands the test of time and resonates with your audience on a deep level. Just like the Israelites trusted Moses to lead them to the promised land, your audience should trust your brand to guide them towards their goals and aspirations. Building a brand is not just about selling products or services; it's about creating a meaningful connection with your audience that lasts a lifetime.

5.4 Collaborations and Joint Ventures: Leveraging Partnerships

Collaborations and joint ventures are powerful strategic tools that entrepreneurs can use to achieve mutual growth and success. By partnering with others, you can leverage each other's strengths and resources to create synergies that benefit both parties involved. In the online world, these collaborations are like modern-day alliances that have the potential to drive your business to new heights.

In the book of Ecclesiastes, it is said that ***"two are better than one, because they have a good reward for their labor."*** This ancient wisdom still holds true today, especially in the fast-paced and competitive world of entrepreneurship. By working together with like-minded individuals or businesses, you can combine your efforts and expertise to achieve greater results than you could on your own.

One of the key benefits of collaborations and joint ventures is the ability to access new markets and audiences. By partnering with another entrepreneur or company, you can tap into their existing customer base and reach a wider audience than you could reach on your own. This can help you expand your business and increase your market share, ultimately leading to greater profitability and success.

Another advantage of collaborations is the opportunity to share resources and expertise. By working with others, you can pool your resources, whether it's financial, technical, or human resources, to achieve common goals. This can help you save time and money, as well as access specialized skills and knowledge that you may not have on your own. By leveraging each other's strengths, you can create a more powerful and efficient business model that benefits all parties involved.

Collaborations and joint ventures also provide opportunities for innovation and creativity. By bringing together different perspectives and ideas, you can create new products, services, or solutions that you may not have been able to develop on your own. This can help you stay ahead of the competition and adapt to changing market trends, ensuring the long-term success and sustainability of your business.

However, it is important to note that collaborations and joint ventures require careful planning and communication to be successful. It is essential to establish clear goals, roles, and expectations from the outset, as well as a mutually beneficial agreement that outlines the terms of the partnership. This can help prevent misunderstandings or conflicts down the line and ensure that both parties are working towards a common objective.

In conclusion, collaborations and joint ventures are powerful tools that entrepreneurs can use to achieve shared success. By working together with others, you can leverage each other's strengths and resources to create synergies that drive your business forward. Remember, "two are better than one," and by partnering with like-minded individuals or businesses, you can achieve greater rewards for your labor. So don't hesitate to explore collaborations and joint ventures as a way to expand your business and reach new heights of success.

5.5 Continuous Learning: Staying Ahead in the Online World

Continuous learning has become increasingly crucial in today's fast-paced and constantly evolving online world. As technology advances and industries change rapidly, it is essential for individuals to stay ahead of the curve by continuously seeking new knowledge and skills. Just as the Israelites fell into complacency and stagnation, so too can individuals in the digital age if they do not make a conscious effort to keep learning and growing.

In the story of Solomon, we see the importance of seeking wisdom and knowledge. Solomon's commitment to learning allowed him to become one of the wisest and most successful rulers in history. Similarly, in the online world, those who prioritize continuous learning are able to adapt to new challenges and opportunities, staying relevant and competitive in their fields. By constantly upgrading their skills and staying informed about industry trends, individuals can position themselves for success in a rapidly changing world.

One of the key benefits of continuous learning is the ability to stay adaptable in the face of change. In today's digital age, industries are constantly evolving, with new technologies and trends emerging regularly. By staying informed and continuously acquiring new knowledge, individuals can better navigate these changes and position themselves for success. Just as the Israelites stumbled when they became complacent, individuals who do not prioritize learning risk falling behind and becoming obsolete in their fields.

Moreover, continuous learning allows individuals to expand their horizons and explore new opportunities. By actively seeking out new knowledge and skills, individuals can discover new passions and interests, opening up new possibilities for personal and professional growth. Just as Solomon's pursuit of wisdom led to his success, so too can a commitment to continuous learning lead to greater opportunities and fulfillment in the online world.

In addition to staying ahead of industry trends, continuous learning also helps individuals to stay innovative and creative. By constantly expanding their knowledge base and exploring new ideas, individuals can approach challenges with fresh perspectives and come up with innovative solutions. Just as Solomon's wisdom allowed him to solve complex problems, so too can continuous learning help individuals to think outside the box and push the boundaries of what is possible in the online world.

Furthermore, continuous learning promotes personal development and lifelong growth. By investing in their education and skill development, individuals can enhance their self-confidence and sense of accomplishment. Just as Solomon's wisdom brought him great renown, so too can continuous learning bring individuals recognition and esteem in their fields. By setting a goal of lifelong learning, individuals can continuously improve themselves and strive for excellence in all aspects of their lives.

The key to successful continuous learning lies in developing a growth mindset. Individuals must be willing to embrace challenges, seek out new experiences, and learn from their mistakes. By cultivating a love of learning and a thirst for knowledge, individuals can create a habit of continuous learning that will serve them well throughout their lives. Just as Solomon's quest for wisdom was never-ending, so too should individuals' pursuit of knowledge be unceasing in order to stay ahead in the online world.

In conclusion, continuous learning is the key to staying ahead in the fast-paced and ever-changing online world. By committing to ongoing education and skill development, individuals can adapt to new challenges, explore new opportunities, stay innovative, and achieve personal growth. Just as Solomon's wisdom brought him success and renown, so too can a commitment to continuous learning bring individuals success and fulfillment in the digital age. By embracing a growth mindset and prioritizing learning, individuals can position themselves for success and stay ahead in an increasingly competitive and dynamic online world.

Climbing to New Heights

In this chapter, you've laid the foundation for scaling your online empire. Just as the Israelites advanced toward the Promised Land, these strategies propel your business toward new horizons. Outsourcing, international expansion, brand building, collaborations, and continuous learning are the steps that lead to exponential growth. Embrace these principles, and you'll ascend to heights previously unimagined in the digital realm.

Chapter 6:

Online Wealth Mindset - Forging Inner Strength for Digital Triumph

6.1 Dealing with Failure and Rejection: Learning from the Wilderness

Dealing with failure and rejection is never easy, but it is an inevitable part of life. Just like the Israelites faced setbacks in the wilderness, we too encounter roadblocks and disappointments along our journey. It is important to remember that these challenges are not meant to break us, but to build us up and shape us into stronger, more resilient individuals.

When we face failure or rejection, it can be easy to become discouraged and lose sight of our goals. We may feel like giving up or believing that we are not good enough. However, just like God provided manna to the Israelites during their testing times, failure can also offer us valuable insights that nourish our growth.

One of the first steps in dealing with failure and rejection is to approach them with a positive mindset. Instead of viewing them as roadblocks, see them as opportunities for growth and self-improvement. Every setback is a chance to learn something new about yourself and your capabilities. It is through failure that we learn what works and what doesn't, what we are good at and what we need to improve on.

Embracing failure also means being open to feedback and constructive criticism. Instead of taking rejection personally, use it as a learning experience to see where you can improve and grow. Seek out mentors or trusted individuals who can provide you with guidance and support during challenging times. Remember, even the most successful individuals have faced failure at some point in their lives. It is how they choose to respond to it that sets them apart.

Another important aspect of dealing with failure is to not dwell on the past. It is easy to get caught up in what could have been or what went wrong. However, constantly replaying past mistakes in your mind only serves to hold you back from moving forward. Instead, focus on the present moment and what you can do today to work towards your goals. Use failure as motivation to push yourself harder and strive for excellence in everything you do.

In addition, it is important to have a support system in place to help you navigate through challenging times. Surround yourself with positive, encouraging individuals who believe in your abilities and can lift you up when you are feeling down. Lean on friends, family, or colleagues for support and guidance during moments of uncertainty. Remember, you are not alone in your journey, and there are people who care about you and want to see you succeed.

Finally, remember to practice self-care and self-compassion during difficult times. It is easy to be hard on yourself when things don't go as planned, but it is important to show yourself kindness and understanding. Treat yourself with the same compassion and forgiveness that you would show to a friend in need. Remember, failure does not define who you are as a person, but how you choose to respond to it does.

In conclusion, dealing with failure and rejection is never easy, but it is a necessary part of growth and self-discovery. Just as the Israelites faced setbacks in the wilderness, we too will encounter challenges along our journey. Embrace failure as a teacher that provides valuable lessons and insights to help you become a better version of yourself. Approach setbacks with a positive mindset, seek out support from others, and practice self-care during difficult times. Remember, you are stronger and more resilient than you think, and you have the power to overcome any obstacle that comes your way.

6.2 Overcoming Procrastination and Self-Doubt: Conquering Inner Canaan

Procrastination and self-doubt are common enemies that we all face at one point or another in our lives. They are like the inner Canaanites that dwell within us, hindering our progress and preventing us from reaching our full potential. Just as Joshua and Caleb overcame their fears and doubts to conquer the Promised Land, we too must learn to conquer our inner Canaan in order to pave the way for success.

Procrastination is often the result of fear or uncertainty. We put off tasks or goals because we are afraid of failure, or because we doubt our ability to succeed. This fear and self-doubt can be paralyzing, preventing us from taking action and moving forward. Just like the Israelites who wandered in the wilderness for 40 years because of their doubts and fears, we too can find ourselves stuck in a cycle of inaction and missed opportunities if we allow procrastination to take hold.

But just as Joshua and Caleb showed courage and determination in the face of adversity, we too can overcome procrastination by harnessing our inner strength and belief in ourselves. We must take a stand against our fears and doubts, and commit to taking the necessary steps towards our goals, no matter how daunting they may seem.

One way to overcome procrastination is to break larger tasks down into smaller, more manageable steps. By setting achievable goals and creating a plan to reach them, we can gradually chip away at our tasks and build momentum towards our ultimate objective. This approach not only makes the task at hand seem less overwhelming, but also allows us to celebrate small victories along the way, boosting our confidence and motivation.

Another effective strategy for overcoming procrastination is to create a sense of accountability. By sharing our goals and progress with others, we are more likely to stay committed and follow through on our actions. Whether it's enlisting the support of a friend or colleague, or joining a group or community that shares similar goals, having a support system in place can help us stay focused and motivated, even when faced with challenges or setbacks.

Self-doubt is another common obstacle that can prevent us from reaching our full potential. It is the voice of insecurity and negativity that whispers in our ear, telling us that we are not capable or worthy of success. Just like the spies who doubted their ability to conquer the Promised Land, we too must learn to silence our inner critics and believe in our own capabilities.

One way to overcome self-doubt is to reframe our thoughts and beliefs about ourselves. Instead of focusing on our perceived limitations or failures, we can shift our mindset towards a more positive and empowering perspective. By reminding ourselves of our past successes and accomplishments, and by setting realistic and achievable goals for the future, we can build a foundation of self-confidence and self-belief that will carry us through even the toughest of challenges.

Practicing self-care and self-compassion is another important aspect of overcoming self-doubt. By prioritizing our physical, mental, and emotional well-being, we can strengthen our resilience and ability to cope with stress and adversity. This includes getting enough rest, exercise, and healthy nutrition, as well as engaging in activities that bring us joy and fulfillment. By taking care of ourselves and nurturing our inner selves, we can cultivate a sense of inner peace and confidence that will help us overcome self-doubt and face any challenge with courage and determination.

In conclusion, procrastination and self-doubt are common obstacles that can hinder our progress and prevent us from reaching our full potential. Just as Joshua and Caleb overcame their fears and doubts to conquer the Promised Land, we too can conquer our inner Canaan by harnessing our determination and self-belief. By breaking tasks down into smaller steps, creating a sense of accountability, reframing our thoughts and beliefs, and practicing self-care and self-compassion, we can overcome procrastination and self-doubt and pave the way for success in all areas of our lives. With courage, determination, and a belief in ourselves, we can conquer our inner Canaan and achieve our goals and dreams.

6.3 Maintaining Work-Life Balance: Embracing the Sabbath of Rest

Maintaining a healthy work-life balance is crucial in today's fast-paced digital world. With constant access to technology and the pressure to always be on, it can be challenging to find time to rest and rejuvenate. However, just like the Sabbath serves as a reminder to take a break and recharge, implementing practices to achieve work-life balance is essential for both personal well-being and professional success.

In the book of Genesis, it is written that God rested on the seventh day after creating the world. This act of rest is not just a religious practice, but a lesson on the importance of taking time to slow down and recharge. In our modern world where work often spills into personal time, it can be easy to forget the value of rest. However, just as God's creativity and productivity flourished after taking a day of rest, so too can ours when we prioritize time for self-care.

Embracing the Sabbath of rest in our own lives can be a transformative practice. Setting aside dedicated time each week to unplug from work and technology allows us to recharge our minds and bodies. This break from the hustle and bustle of daily life gives us the opportunity to reflect, relax, and connect with ourselves and our loved ones. By creating boundaries around work and personal time, we can better prioritize our mental health and well-being.

Striking a balance between work and personal life is not just important for our own happiness, but also for our professional success. Research has shown that burnout and overwork can lead to decreased productivity, creativity, and overall job satisfaction. By taking the time to rest and recharge, we can actually become more productive and efficient in our work. When we are well-rested and mentally refreshed, we are better able to focus, problem-solve, and think creatively.

In order to maintain a healthy work-life balance, it is important to set boundaries and prioritize self-care. This may involve establishing a regular routine for rest and relaxation, such as scheduling time for exercise, hobbies, or spending time with loved ones. It may also involve setting boundaries around work hours, such as turning off email notifications after a certain time or setting aside specific days to be completely off work.

In addition to setting boundaries, it is important to practice mindfulness and self-awareness in our daily lives. This may involve taking breaks throughout the day to rest and recharge, practicing deep breathing or meditation, or simply being present in the moment. By cultivating a sense of mindfulness and self-awareness, we can better manage stress, improve our focus, and increase our overall well-being.

Ultimately, maintaining work-life balance is about prioritizing our own well-being and happiness. It is about recognizing that our mental, emotional, and physical health are just as important as our professional success. By embracing the Sabbath of rest in our own lives, we can create a sustainable foundation for success and fulfillment. Just as God rested on the seventh day, so too should we take time to rest and rejuvenate in order to thrive in our personal and professional lives.

6.4 Cultivating Resilience and Persistence: Echoes of Endurance

The journey of the Israelites through trials and tribulations in the wilderness serves as a powerful reminder of the resilience and persistence required in any online venture. Just as they faced numerous obstacles and setbacks on their journey towards the promised land, so too will you encounter challenges and difficulties in your quest for success in the digital world.

Cultivating resilience is essential for overcoming the inevitable hurdles that will come your way. It involves developing a mindset that allows you to bounce back from setbacks and failures, and to keep moving forward despite the obstacles in your path. Resilience is not just about staying strong in the face of adversity; it is also about being flexible and adaptable, willing to change course when necessary and to learn from your mistakes.

Persistence is another key trait that the Israelites demonstrated in their journey through the wilderness. Despite facing countless trials and hardships, they continued to press on towards their goal, refusing to give up in the face of seemingly insurmountable challenges. Similarly, in the world of online business, persistence is crucial for achieving success. It requires a willingness to keep pushing forward, even when things are difficult, and to remain focused on your goals despite the obstacles in your way.

The story of the Israelites' journey through the wilderness is a powerful example of the endurance and perseverance that are required to succeed in any endeavor. It serves as a reminder that success rarely comes easily, and that the path to achievement is often filled with obstacles and challenges. However, just as the Israelites eventually reached the promised land after enduring years of hardship, so too can you overcome the challenges in your online venture and achieve your goals with determination and persistence.

One of the key lessons from the Israelites' journey is the importance of faith and trust in the face of adversity. Despite facing numerous trials and tribulations, the Israelites continued to trust in the promises of their God and to have faith that they would eventually reach their destination. In the same way, in the world of online business, it is important to have faith in your abilities and to trust that you will eventually achieve success, even when things seem bleak.

Another important lesson from the Israelites' journey is the need for perseverance in the face of setbacks. Despite facing numerous obstacles and challenges, the Israelites refused to give up on their goal and continued to press on towards the promised land. Similarly, in the world of online business, it is important to persevere in the face of difficulties and to remain committed to your goals, even when the going gets tough.

In conclusion, the story of the Israelites' journey through the wilderness serves as a powerful reminder of the resilience and persistence required to succeed in any online venture. By cultivating these traits and remaining steadfast in the face of challenges, you can weather the storms of entrepreneurship and emerge stronger on the other side. Just as the Israelites eventually reached the promised land after enduring years of hardship, so too can you achieve success in the digital world by echoing their endurance and determination.

6.5 Celebrating Success: The Importance of Gratitude

Celebrating success is an important aspect of life that often goes unnoticed. Too often, we are focused on the next goal or milestone, without taking the time to acknowledge and appreciate the accomplishments we have already achieved. However, taking the time to celebrate success with gratitude can have a profound impact on our journey and overall well-being.

Just as the Israelites praised God for their triumphs, we too should take the time to acknowledge and express gratitude for our successes. By doing so, we fortify our journey and build a strong foundation for future endeavors. When we celebrate our successes with gratitude, we are able to recognize the hard work, dedication, and perseverance that went into achieving our goals. This not only serves as a reminder of our capabilities but also fuels our motivation to continue striving for greatness.

Acknowledging our accomplishments with gratitude can help cultivate a positive mindset. When we focus on the things we have achieved rather than the things we have yet to accomplish, we are able to shift our perspective and appreciate the progress we have made. This positive mindset can have a ripple effect on other areas of our lives, leading to increased confidence, resilience, and overall happiness.

Gratitude is a powerful tool that can enhance our capacity for future successes. When we express gratitude for the achievements we have made, we are able to recognize the support and resources that helped us along the way. This sense of appreciation can foster a sense of abundance and attract more opportunities for success into our lives. By cultivating a mindset of gratitude, we are able to approach challenges with a sense of optimism and confidence, knowing that we have the ability to overcome obstacles and achieve our goals.

In conclusion, celebrating success with gratitude is a powerful practice that can have a profound impact on our journey. Just as the Israelites praised God for their triumphs, we too should take the time to acknowledge and express gratitude for our accomplishments. By doing so, we build a strong foundation for future endeavors, cultivate a positive mindset, and enhance our capacity for future successes. So, let us take the time to celebrate our successes with gratitude, and watch as our journey unfolds with abundance and joy.

Forging Inner Strength

In this chapter, we've delved into the inner world of the online wealth mindset. Dealing with failure, overcoming self-doubt, maintaining balance, cultivating resilience, and celebrating success are the pillars of inner strength. Just as the Israelites' mindset shaped their destiny, your mindset will determine your digital triumph. Embrace these principles to forge the unyielding mindset required for success in the online world.

Chapter 7:

Legal and Ethical Considerations - Navigating the Moral Compass of Online Entrepreneurship

7.1 Understanding Online Laws and Regulations: A Digital Covenant

In the digital age, navigating the complex landscape of online laws and regulations is essential for businesses and individuals alike. Just as the Israelites were guided by the laws of the land, understanding and complying with digital laws can be seen as a modern-day covenant that shapes the way we engage with the online world. By adhering to legal requirements, businesses can protect themselves from potential legal consequences and build trust with their customers. Similarly, considering online regulations as a guiding principle can help individuals operate within ethical boundaries and contribute to a safer and more responsible online environment.

The importance of understanding and abiding by online laws and regulations cannot be overstated in today's interconnected world. With the rapid advancement of technology and the increasing reliance on digital platforms for communication, commerce, and social interaction, the legal framework governing the online sphere has become more intricate and expansive. From data privacy and cybersecurity to intellectual property rights and e-commerce regulations, there are a myriad of laws that businesses and individuals must comply with to operate legally and ethically in the digital realm.

Just as the Israelites were governed by divine laws that provided them with a moral compass and guidelines for living harmoniously within their community, adhering to online laws and regulations serves a similar purpose in the digital age. These laws are designed to protect the rights and interests of individuals, safeguard sensitive information, prevent fraud and abuse, and promote fair competition in the online marketplace. By understanding and complying with these regulations, businesses can demonstrate their commitment to ethical practices, earn the trust of their customers and stakeholders, and avoid costly legal repercussions.

Moreover, viewing online laws and regulations as a digital covenant can help individuals and businesses navigate the complexities of the digital landscape with integrity and accountability. Just as the Israelites upheld their covenant with God as a sacred agreement, honoring legal requirements in the online space signifies a commitment to upholding principles of fairness, transparency, and responsibility. By treating online regulations as a moral code that guides their actions and decisions, individuals can foster a culture of trust and respect in online interactions, contributing to a more secure and trustworthy digital environment for all.

In conclusion, understanding and complying with online laws and regulations is crucial for businesses and individuals to navigate the complexities of the digital world responsibly and ethically. Just as the Israelites were guided by the laws of the land, viewing online regulations as a digital covenant can help establish a framework for operating within legal boundaries and fostering trust with stakeholders. By upholding legal requirements, businesses can protect themselves from legal risks and demonstrate their commitment to ethical conduct. Likewise, individuals can contribute to a safer and more respectful online community by honoring online laws as a guiding principle that shapes their online behavior. Ultimately, treating online regulations as a digital covenant can lead to a more compliant, trustworthy, and secure online environment for everyone.

7.2 Protecting Intellectual Property: Safeguarding Your Digital Inheritance

Protecting intellectual property is crucial in safeguarding your digital inheritance for future generations. Just as King Solomon's wisdom ensured the prosperity of his kingdom, securing your creations ensures that your hard work and innovation are respected and preserved. Whether you are an artist, writer, inventor, or entrepreneur, intellectual property rights are essential in protecting your ideas and creations from being unlawfully used or copied by others.

Intellectual property refers to creations of the mind, such as inventions, literary and artistic works, designs, symbols, names, and images used in commerce. These creations are protected by various laws and regulations to ensure that their creators have the exclusive rights to use, reproduce, and distribute them. By safeguarding your intellectual property, you not only protect your own interests but also contribute to the overall climate of innovation and creativity in society.

One of the key ways to protect intellectual property is through copyright, which grants authors, artists, and other creators the exclusive rights to reproduce, distribute, and display their works. Copyright protection applies to various forms of creative expression, including books, music, art, and software. By obtaining copyright protection for your work, you can prevent others from using or copying it without your permission.

Trademarks are another important form of intellectual property protection, used to protect symbols, names, and logos that identify and distinguish products and services in the marketplace. By registering a trademark for your business name or logo, you can prevent competitors from using similar marks that could confuse consumers or dilute your brand identity.

Patents are another crucial form of intellectual property protection, granting inventors exclusive rights to their inventions for a specified period of time. By obtaining a patent for your invention, you can prevent others from producing, selling, or using it without your permission. Patents encourage innovation by rewarding inventors for their creativity and investment in developing new technologies.

Trade secrets are another key component of intellectual property protection, used to safeguard valuable proprietary information that gives a company a competitive advantage in the marketplace. By implementing measures to protect trade secrets, such as confidentiality agreements and restricted access to sensitive information, businesses can prevent competitors from gaining access to their valuable intellectual assets.

In today's digital age, intellectual property protection is more important than ever, as the internet has made it easier for individuals and companies to access, copy, and distribute digital content without authorization. Piracy and copyright infringement are common challenges faced by creators and businesses, leading to revenue loss and reputational damage. By taking proactive measures to protect your intellectual property online, such as using encryption, digital rights management tools, and copyright notices, you can reduce the risk of unauthorized use and ensure that your creations are respected and valued.

In conclusion, safeguarding your intellectual property is essential in protecting your digital inheritance and ensuring that your ideas and creations are respected and preserved for future generations. By obtaining copyright, trademarks, patents, and trade secret protection for your intellectual assets, you can prevent unauthorized use and exploitation of your work, while fostering a culture of innovation and creativity in society. Just as King Solomon's wisdom secured his kingdom, protecting your intellectual property ensures that your legacy will endure and thrive in the digital age.

7.3 Maintaining Ethical Standards: Walking in Integrity

Maintaining ethical standards is a foundational principle that should guide every aspect of our lives. Just as the Ten Commandments served as a set of rules for the Israelites to follow, ethical standards provide a framework for how we should behave and make decisions in our personal and professional lives. At the core of ethical standards is the concept of integrity, which is the quality of being honest and having strong moral principles. When we uphold ethical standards, we are demonstrating to others that we can be trusted and relied upon to act in a principled manner.

One of the key ethical principles outlined in the Ten Commandments is the prohibition against stealing. This commandment serves as a reminder that taking something that does not belong to us is not only unethical but also morally wrong. When we steal, we are not only harming the person from whom we are taking, but we are also compromising our own integrity and character. By refraining from stealing, we are demonstrating our respect for the property and rights of others, as well as upholding the principles of honesty and justice.

Another important ethical principle outlined in the commandments is the prohibition against bearing false witness against our neighbor. This commandment reminds us that spreading lies or misinformation about others is not only harmful but also unethical. When we bear false witness, we are damaging the reputation and credibility of another person, as well as violating their right to be treated with fairness and respect. By refraining from spreading falsehoods about others, we are upholding the principles of truthfulness and integrity, and demonstrating our commitment to ethical behavior.

In today's digital age, maintaining ethical standards is more important than ever. With the rise of social media and online communication, it is easier than ever for information to be shared and spread rapidly. This means that our actions and decisions can have a far-reaching impact, not only on our own lives but also on the lives of others. By upholding ethical standards in our online interactions, we can build trust and credibility with our audience, as well as demonstrate our commitment to acting with integrity and honesty.

One of the key ways to maintain ethical standards in our digital interactions is to be mindful of the information we share and the way we present ourselves online. This means refraining from spreading false information or engaging in gossip and rumors, as well as being cautious about the information we share about ourselves and others. By taking the time to verify the accuracy of the information we share and ensuring that it aligns with our values and principles, we can avoid inadvertently compromising our integrity and reputation.

In addition to being mindful of the information we share online, it is also important to be respectful and considerate in our interactions with others. This means treating others with kindness and compassion, as well as refraining from engaging in behaviors that are hurtful or offensive. By practicing empathy and understanding in our online interactions, we can build positive relationships with others and create a culture of respect and decency in our digital communities.

Maintaining ethical standards also means being transparent and honest in our communications and relationships. This means being upfront about our intentions and motivations, as well as being willing to admit when we have made a mistake or acted inappropriately. By being open and honest in our interactions, we can build trust and credibility with others, as well as demonstrate our commitment to acting with integrity and authenticity.

Ultimately, maintaining ethical standards is about walking in integrity and living according to our core values and principles. By upholding ethical standards in our actions and decisions, we can build credibility and trust with others, as well as demonstrate our commitment to acting with honesty and integrity. Just as the commandments guided the Israelites in their conduct, ethical standards serve as our digital commandments, guiding us in how we should behave and interact with others in the digital age. By embracing ethical standards and walking in integrity, we can create a more ethical, honest, and compassionate digital world for ourselves and others.

7.4 Building Trust with Customers and Partners: The Foundation of Covenant

Building trust with customers and partners is essential for the long-term success of any business. Just as God's faithfulness was the foundation of the Israelites' relationship, your trustworthiness forms the bedrock of your business relationships. By consistently delivering on promises and fostering open and transparent communication, you can cultivate strong and lasting relationships with your customers and partners.

Trust is the cornerstone of any successful business relationship. When customers and partners trust you, they are more likely to do business with you, recommend your products or services to others, and continue to work with you in the future. Trust is earned through a combination of integrity, reliability, competence, and honesty.

Integrity is the foundation of trust. When you operate with integrity, you are honest, ethical, and transparent in all of your dealings. You are true to your word and you do what you say you will do. This consistency builds trust over time, as customers and partners can rely on you to act with integrity in all situations.

Reliability is another key component of trust. When you are reliable, you consistently deliver on your promises and commitments. You follow through on your word, meet deadlines, and deliver high-quality products or services. When customers and partners can rely on you to do what you say you will do, they are more likely to trust you and continue to do business with you.

Competence is also important when building trust with customers and partners. You must demonstrate that you have the knowledge, skills, and experience to meet their needs and deliver value. By consistently delivering high-quality products or services and providing expert advice and guidance, you can establish yourself as a trusted and competent partner.

Honesty is another crucial element of trust. You must be transparent and truthful in all of your communications and dealings with customers and partners. If there are any issues or challenges, you must be honest about them and work to resolve them in a timely and effective manner. By being honest and transparent, you can build trust and credibility with your customers and partners.

In order to build trust with customers and partners, it is important to focus on communication. Open and transparent communication is key to building strong and lasting relationships. You must keep customers and partners informed about your products or services, updates, changes, and any issues that may arise. By keeping the lines of communication open, you can build trust and confidence with your customers and partners.

Listening is also an important aspect of communication when building trust with customers and partners. You must listen to their needs, concerns, and feedback in order to understand their perspective and address their issues. By actively listening to your customers and partners, you can demonstrate that you value their input and are committed to building a strong and mutually beneficial relationship.

Building trust with customers and partners is an ongoing process that requires time, effort, and dedication. It is important to consistently demonstrate integrity, reliability, competence, honesty, and open communication in all of your interactions. By building trust with your customers and partners, you can establish a solid foundation for a successful and long-lasting business relationship. Trust is the key to building strong and lasting relationships with customers and partners, and should be nurtured and maintained over time. By focusing on integrity, reliability, competence, honesty, and open communication, you can build trust with your customers and partners and establish a strong foundation for a successful business relationship.

7.5 Resolving Disputes and Handling Legal Issues: Wisdom in Resolution

Resolving disputes and handling legal issues in a business setting requires a level of wisdom that mirrors the famed judgment of King Solomon. Just as Solomon's wisdom brought harmony and resolution to conflicts, addressing disputes with fairness and equitability can lead to positive outcomes that maintain relationships and uphold the principles of justice.

In today's fast-paced and interconnected business world, disputes and legal issues are bound to arise. Whether it's a disagreement between business partners, a contractual dispute with a vendor, or a legal challenge from a competitor, how these conflicts are resolved can have a significant impact on the reputation and success of a business.

One key principle to keep in mind when resolving disputes is the importance of fairness and justice. Just as Solomon was known for his wise judgment in the biblical story of the two women who claimed to be the mother of the same child, a business leader should strive to be fair and impartial when dealing with conflicts. This can involve listening to all parties involved, considering all the facts and evidence, and making decisions based on what is right and just.

Another important aspect of resolving disputes with wisdom is the ability to maintain relationships while finding a resolution. In business, maintaining positive relationships with clients, partners, and stakeholders is essential for long-term success. By approaching disputes with a focus on preserving these relationships, a business leader can help ensure that conflicts are resolved in a way that is mutually beneficial and fosters trust and cooperation.

Handling legal issues in a business setting also requires a high level of integrity and respect. Legal challenges can be complex and daunting, but by approaching them with honesty and transparency, a business can navigate these challenges in a way that upholds the principles of ethical conduct and legal compliance.

The biblical verse from Proverbs 10:8 highlights the importance of wisdom in decision-making. The wise in heart are those who are open to receiving guidance and counsel, and who are willing to consider different perspectives before making a decision. In contrast, the prating fool is someone who is arrogant and closed-minded, and who is quick to make decisions without considering the consequences.

In the context of resolving disputes and handling legal issues in a business setting, this verse serves as a reminder of the importance of humility, openness, and the willingness to seek advice and counsel from others. By approaching conflicts with a humble and open heart, a business leader can increase the likelihood of finding a wise and equitable resolution that is in the best interests of all parties involved.

In conclusion, resolving disputes and handling legal issues in a business setting requires a high level of wisdom, integrity, and respect. By approaching conflicts with fairness, equitability, and a focus on maintaining relationships, a business leader can navigate challenges in a way that upholds the principles of justice and ethics. Just as Solomon's wisdom brought harmony and resolution to conflicts, so too can a business leader's wise judgment lead to positive outcomes that benefit all parties involved.

Upholding Virtue in the Digital Realm

In this chapter, you've journeyed through the moral compass of online entrepreneurship. Understanding laws, protecting intellectual property, maintaining ethical standards, building trust, and handling disputes are the pillars of virtue in the digital realm. Just as the Israelites adhered to divine principles, your commitment to ethical practices sets the tone for your online legacy. Embrace these considerations to navigate the digital landscape with integrity and purpose.

Chapter 8

Conclusion - Embarking on Your Digital Odyssey to Online Millions

As you stand at the threshold of this concluding chapter, you're armed with knowledge, strategies, and the wisdom of ages past. Your journey through *"Unlocking Online Wealth: Strategies for Making Millions Online"* has been a voyage of discovery, inspiration, and empowerment. Just as the Israelites crossed the Jordan River to enter the Promised Land, you're poised to step into the realm of online success.

The Digital Promised Land Beckons

The digital Promised Land is not just a place of financial abundance, but a state of mind where innovation, creativity, and growth converge. The online world is your canvas, and your actions are the brushstrokes that shape your destiny. Your passion, combined with the principles outlined in this book, forms the blueprint for building your online empire.

Embrace the Challenges and Triumphs

Remember that like any journey, your path to online millions will be marked by challenges and triumphs. Just as the Israelites encountered obstacles and miracles on their journey, your road will be a mix of setbacks and victories. Embrace these experiences as opportunities for growth, learning, and transformation.

Unleash Your Potential

The potential of the online world is boundless. Just as the Israelites found sustenance in the wilderness, you have a plethora of resources, tools, and platforms at your disposal. Your success is limited only by your vision, dedication, and willingness to adapt.

Your Journey Begins Now

As you close this chapter and turn the page, remember that your journey to online millions begins now. Armed with a wealth of knowledge and insights, step into the digital landscape with confidence and purpose. Seize opportunities, innovate, and let the principles outlined in this book guide you.

May your digital odyssey be marked by innovation, growth, and prosperity. As you navigate the online realm, may you find fulfillment in both financial success and the impact you create. With the wisdom of the ages as your guide, set forth on your path to making millions online.

Wishing you great success and prosperity on your journey,

[Prophet PD John]

Bibliography:

1. Timothy Ferriss (2007), The 4-Hour Work Week, Crown Publishers, New York

2. Gary Vaynerchuk (2009), Crush It!: Why Now Is the Time to Cash in on Your Passion, HarperStudio, New York

3. Pat Flynn (2016), Will It Fly?: How to Test Your Next Business Idea So You Don't Waste Your Time and Money, CreateSpace Independent Publishing Platform, Scotts Valley

4. Ramit Sethi (2009), I Will Teach You to Be Rich, Workman Publishing Company, New York

5. Neil Patel (2019), Digital Marketing for Dummies, For Dummies, Hoboken

6. Larry Kim (2018), The Definitive Guide to Google AdWords: Create Versatile and Powerful Marketing and Advertising Campaigns, Independently published, Lexington

7. Jenna Kutcher (2019), The Essential Habits of 6-Figure Bloggers: Secrets of 17 Successful Bloggers

You Can Use to Build a Six-Figure Online Business, Independently published, Ames

8. Ash Maurya (2012), Running Lean: Iterate from Plan A to a Plan That Works, O'Reilly Media, Inc., Sebastopol

9. John Jantsch (2018), Duct Tape Marketing: The World's Most Practical Small Business Marketing Guide, Portfolio, New York

10. Maria Forleo (2019), Everything is Figureoutable, Portfolio, New York.

OTHER BOOKS

BY PROPHET PD JOHN

1. Level 1 Prophetic Training Manual

Available at .Amazon.cm, Barnes & Noble, Saxo.com, Goodreads etc...

2. Level 2 Prophetic Training Manual

Available at .Amazon.cm, Barnes & Noble, Saxo.com, Goodreads etc...

3. Level 3 Prophetic Training Manual: Advanced Prophetic Training

Available at .Amazon.cm, Barnes & Noble, Saxo.com, Goodreads etc...

4. Level 4 Prophetic Training Manual: The Ultimate Training in Prophetic

Available at .Amazon.cm, Barnes & Noble, Saxo.com, Goodreads etc...

5. Archangel Uriel: The Keeper of Divine Light

Available at .Amazon.cm, Barnes & Noble, Saxo.com, Goodreads etc...

6. **7 Reasons Some Church Ministers Associate with Freemasons.**

Available at .Amazon.cm, Barnes & Noble, Saxo.com, Goodreads etc...

7. **Archangel Michael: the warrior angel,**

Available at .Amazon.cm, Barnes & Noble, Saxo.com, Goodreads etc...

8. Battle Between Godly and Satanic Altars

Available at .Amazon.cm, Barnes & Noble, Saxo.com, Goodreads etc...

9. Dorah & The Dragons: A Fantasy Tale for Children

Available at .Amazon.cm, Barnes & Noble, Saxo.com, Goodreads etc...

10. Dreams and Interpretations: Understanding The Dream World

Available at .Amazon.cm, Barnes & Noble, Saxo.com, Goodreads etc...

11. SECRETS TO ENTER THE KINGDOM OF HEAVEN

Available at .Amazon.cm, Barnes & Noble, Saxo.com, Goodreads etc...

12. How to Meditate Effectively

Available at .Amazon.cm, Barnes & Noble, Saxo.com, Goodreads etc...

13. Mystery of Christmas Day Unveiled

Available at .Amazon.cm, Barnes & Noble, Saxo.com, Goodreads etc...

14. Train Up Your Child in the Way He Should Go

Available at .Amazon.cm, Barnes & Noble, Saxo.com, Goodreads etc...

15. Guide to Dream Journaling

Available at .Amazon.cm, Barnes & Noble, Saxo.com, Goodreads etc...

16. How to Raise the Dead

Available at .Amazon.cm, Barnes & Noble, Saxo.com, Goodreads etc...

17. How to Go Through The Process Of Spiritual Growth

Available at .Amazon.cm, Barnes & Noble, Saxo.com, Goodreads etc...

18. Holy Spirity

Available at .Amazon.cm, Barnes & Noble, Saxo.com, Goodreads etc...

19. How to Pray Against Monitoring Spirity

Available at .Amazon.cm, Barnes & Noble, Saxo.com, Goodreads etc...

20. Jonah The Prophet:The Burden of the Prophetic Calling

Available at .Amazon.cm, Barnes & Noble, Saxo.com, Goodreads etc...

21. Exploring The Art of Reasoning

Available at .Amazon.cm, Barnes & Noble, Saxo.com, Goodreads etc...

22. Mystery Behind Praise And Worship

Available at .Amazon.cm, Barnes & Noble, Saxo.com, Goodreads etc...

23. Level 1 Christian Seers Training Manual

Available at .Amazon.cm, Barnes & Noble, Saxo.com, Goodreads etc...

24. TITLE - LEVEL 2 CHRISTIAN SEERS TRAINING MANUAL

Available at .Amazon.cm, Barnes & Noble, Saxo.com, Goodreads etc...

25. **TITLE - LEVEL 3 CHRISTIAN SEERS TRAINING MANUAL**

Available at .Amazon.cm, Barnes & Noble, Saxo.com, Goodreads etc...

26. **TITLE - LEVEL 4 CHRISTIAN SEERS TRAINING MANUAL: ULTIMATE TRAINING IN THE SEER MINISTRY**

Available at .Amazon.cm, Barnes & Noble, Saxo.com, Goodreads etc...

27. The Azusa Street Revival: Awakening the Spirit Within

Available at .Amazon.cm, Barnes & Noble, Saxo.com, Goodreads etc...

28. THE HEART OF A SPIRITUAL FATHER

Available at .Amazon.cm, Barnes & Noble, Saxo.com, Goodreads etc...

www.ingramcontent.com/pod-product-compliance
Lightning Source LLC
Chambersburg PA
CBHW071925210526
45479CB00002B/565